Make Your Own Art

Card Making

Sally Henry

PowerKiDS press.

New York

Published in 2009 by The Rosen Publishing Group, Inc.
29 East 21st Street, New York, NY 10010

Copyright © 2009 Arcturus Publishing Ltd. First published in
2008 by Franklin Watts.

Editor: Alex Woolf
Designers: Sally Henry and Trevor Cook
Consultant: Daisy Fearns
U.S. Editor: Kara Murray

Picture credits: Sally Henry and Trevor Cook

Every attempt has been made to clear copyright. Should there
be any inadvertent omission, please apply to the publisher
for rectification.

Library of Congress Cataloging-in-Publication Data

Henry, Sally.
  Card making / Sally Henry.
    p. cm. — (Make your own art)
  Includes index.
  ISBN 978-1-4358-2506-2 (library binding)
ISBN 978-1-4358-2639-7 (pbk)
ISBN 978-1-4358-2651-9 (6-pack)
  1. Greeting card—Juvenile literature. I. Title.
  TT872.H46 2009
  745.594'1—dc22

                                        2008004326

Manufactured in China

Contents

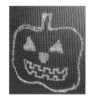

Introduction

Greeting cards

A greeting card is always more welcome when it has been made by the person sending it. In this book you'll find lots of ways to make your cards even more special.

Paper and card stock

You need a supply of colored paper and card stock.

Paper: All sizes are useful.

Card stock: It's important for your card to stand up and keep its shape. Larger cards have to be made from thicker card stock.

Folding and cutting

In our instructions, we use a dotted line to show a **fold** and a solid line for a **cut**. There's usually a fold or an edge that the folded part has to meet.

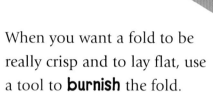

fold line

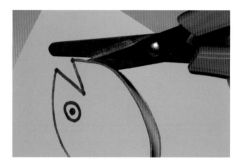

cutting along a line

When you want a fold to be really crisp and to lay flat, use a tool to **burnish** the fold.

Safety first

Always ask an adult to help you when you are using sharp objects, such as scissors or thumbtacks.

burnishing a fold

Glue

glue stick

There are three kinds of glue you may need. The kind that comes as a **glue stick** is ideal for glueing card stock and paper. Place the piece to be glued face down on a clean piece of scrap paper and apply the glue evenly, working from the middle towards the edge. Spread the glue right onto the scrap paper. There shouldn't be any extra or blobs on the front.

White glue will stick paper and card stock together well, but it is best not to spread it over a large area. It's good for drawing with glitter (see page 27).

Rubber cement can come in a tube and is best for sticking odd-shaped things or unusual materials together. It can become stringy, so test it on scrap first.

rubber cement

white craft glue

Presentation

It's great to be able to give your friends a beautiful, unusual or funny greeting card that you've made yourself. We've got lots of designs to choose from. There are shaped and three-dimensional as well as regular ones. You can use paint, pens or collage to make your cards.

Design

All the designs in this book are based on something that will fold up and fit into an envelope. It's very important that your finished card fit, so it's a good idea to have the envelope ready when you start working.

Standard envelopes

For most projects an ordinary envelope will do for your card. You can get colored ones from craft shops. They are often made in unusual shapes, so shop around. If you want a special size and you can't find it, you can make your own using the simple guide opposite.

Make your own envelopes

In the picture we've shown the shape of the finished paper (orange). You will need to make the envelope (red). You can change this design for different shapes of envelope. Ask an adult to help you with cutting out the diamond shape. Make sure you cut the curved parts exactly as shown.

Finish the envelope as follows:

- Fold the bottom part up.
- Fold the side parts, glue their lower edges to the bottom parts.
- Fold the top part down.

Don't stick the top part down until you have put your card inside!

a

— trip of glue

The red shape is the size of the inside of your envelope. Put it in the middle of the diamond.

c

d

b

The distance from a to b is twice the height of the red shape plus 1 inch (25 mm). The distance from c to d is twice the width of the red shape plus 1 inch (25 mm).

Birthday Cake

Celebrate a special birthday with this cake and candles card.

You will need:

- Colored paper
- Thin white card stock
- Corrugated paper
- Scissors, glue stick
- Large envelope

35 MINUTES

What to do...

Fold your white card stock into a tent shape. Use more white card stock for the candles. Choose brightly colored papers to make the cut-out shapes.

5 MINUTES

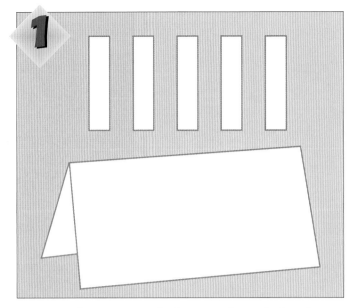

Cut out thin strips of white card stock for the candles. Make as many as you need.

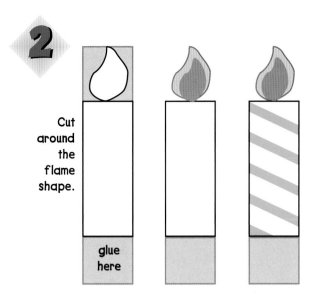

Cut out a flame shape at the top of each candle. Glue on the colored paper flames and stripes.

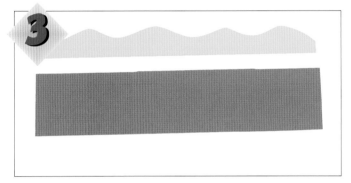

Cut a rectangular shape for the cake band and a wavy shape for the frosting. Glue them on.

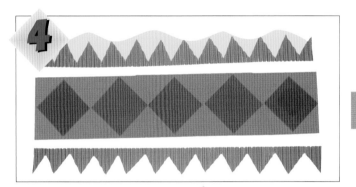

Cut some zigzag strips and diamond shapes and glue them in position (see opposite page).

Glue the candles to the back of the card. Space them out evenly. The card is complete!

Write your greeting inside the card. If you need to make a special envelope, see page 7.

Tortoise and Hare

Making this design is very quick, but make sure you follow the instructions carefully! We've made hares and tortoises, but you can try any animals to make your cards.

You will need:

- *Colored papers*
- *Scissors*
- *Glue stick*
- *Pencil and markers*
- *Envelopes*

20
MINUTES

What to do...

Always make sharp exact folds in your paper. Cut as neatly as you can to give smooth edges to your cards. Always make sure you're not cutting the joining parts on the fold!

5
MINUTES

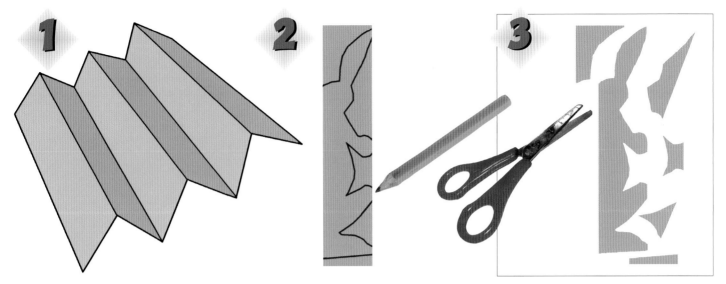

1 Fold your paper lengthwise in six parts to make a zigzag.

2 To make three hares, mark the shapes as shown above.

3 Keep the paper folded and cut out the shapes.

4 Open your card out. Now we need some details.

5 Cut out three bow ties in different colors.

6 Glue them on. Cut out and glue on noses, eyes and whiskers.

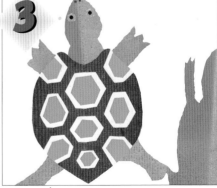

1 Repeat the method. This time we're making tortoises!

2 Mark the shapes with a pencil. Cut out with scissors and open.

3 Decorate the shells. Don't forget the greeting on the back!

Stamp Designs

35 MINUTES

5 MINUTES

12

Stamped designs are simple but quick and fun to make. You can change your stamps to fit the occasion or the person the card is for.

You will need:

- Colored card stock, envelopes
- Spongy kitchen cloth
- Plastic lids
- Scissors, rubber cement
- Markers
- Paintbrush
- Poster paints
- Tissues for cleaning up

What to do...

Draw some simple shapes on paper or directly onto some spongy cloth. Our card has frogs, water lilies and ducks. Copy the templates on the opposite page or you can draw your own designs. Make sure your image will fit on the flat side of your lid. After you have finished, wash your stamps under the tap and keep them for next time.

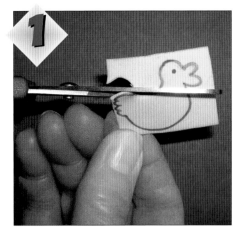

Draw shapes on spongy cloth and cut them out.

You can use paper patterns if you find it easier.

Glue the shapes onto a plastic lid and allow the glue to dry.

Use thick poster paint to cover the raised part of your stamp.

Turn the lid over and press the stamp on to the card.

Lift off to show the first image. Repeat from step 3.

13

Work from left to right so that you don't smudge your work (or right to left if you are left-handed). Let the paint dry.

Make up more stamps to finish your card.

You can use half of a potato to make a stamp. Carefully cut patterns on the flat side. Ask an adult to help.

Button Badges

Your friends will be delighted if you give them badges. Create unusual card badges with safety pins. It's easy! Just follow steps 1 to 4.

You will need:

- *Thin card stock, needle and thread*
- *Colored felt, colored paper*
- *Buttons, safety pins, pencil*
- *Scissors, envelopes*

25 MINUTES

What to do...

Sort out your materials into sets of three colors that look good together.

5 MINUTES

1 Draw and cut out some flower shapes in different colored felt or a similar material.

2 Try different shapes and colors together. Use curves, zigzags and borders.

3 Choose a colored button for each badge. Sew the button on with a needle and thread to keep all the shapes together.

4 Sew a safety pin to the back of each badge. Pin the badges to folded cards. Use them for your party invitations or just for fun!

some ideas for badges with two buttons

Birthday Clowns

45 MINUTES

5 MINUTES

16

You will need:

- Colored card stock, a large envelope
- Scissors, glue stick, a thumbtack
- Markers and a pencil
- 5 paper fasteners, string, glitter
- Plastic wobbly eyes (optional)

What to do...

Copy or trace the shapes opposite onto colored card stock, then cut them out. Decorate the shapes with glued-on colored paper or draw in the details with markers. Check that the completed card fits the envelope.

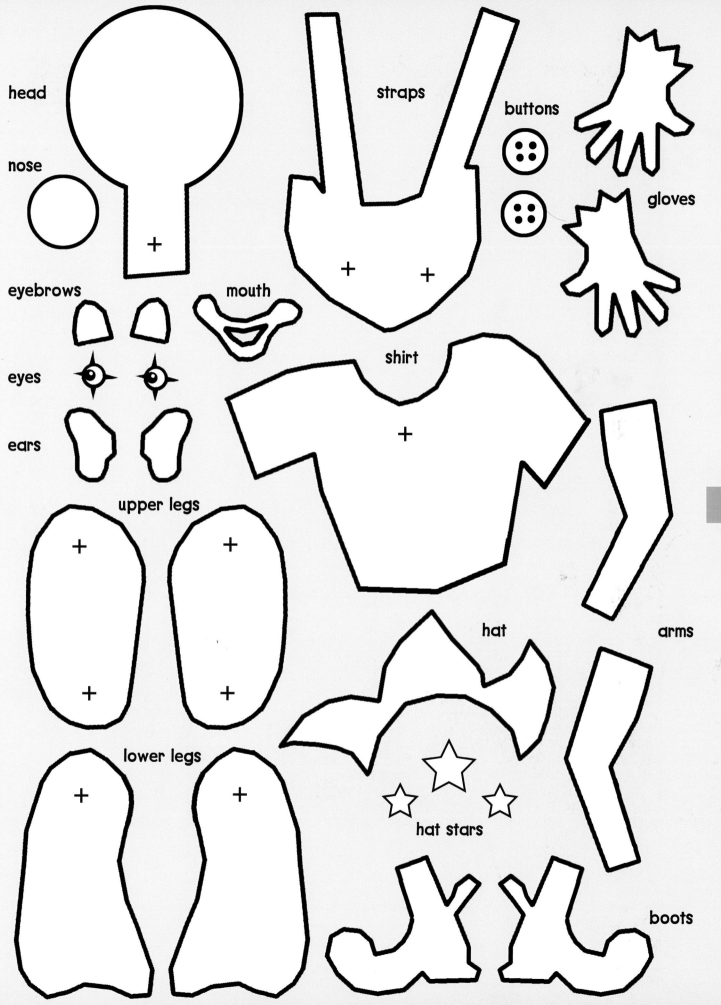

head

nose

straps

buttons

gloves

eyebrows

mouth

eyes

shirt

ears

upper legs

hat

arms

lower legs

hat stars

boots

17

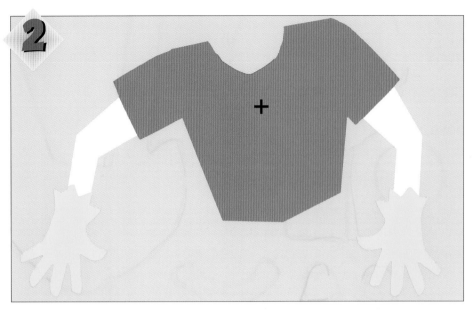

1 Find his head shape and stick his hat on. Glue on his nose, eyebrows, eyes and mouth. Stick on his ears, then put the stars on his hat!

2 Find his arms, two gloves and shirt. Stick his arms behind his shirt and his gloves over his arms as shown.

You will see crosses (+) on the template shapes. These show where you should make a small hole with a thumbtack. The holes are for paper fasteners.

Paper fastener

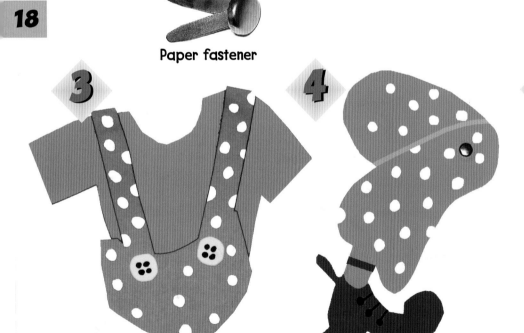

3 Glue the straps over his shirt. Stick on both the buttons. Allow it to dry.

4 Glue his boots to the lower halves of the pants and point them left and right! Connect his upper legs to his lower legs using paper fasteners.

5 With more fasteners, join his legs to his body, then join his head to his shirt. Add a string loop to his hat.

Make sure you haven't left any pieces out. Write a greeting on the back of your clown. Swing his arms and legs around to fit in a big envelope (see page 7) and address it to your friend.

Fairy

Robot

Pirate

Here are some other faces to copy if you want to make more fun birthday cards. They will also make great party invitations. Write all the details about the party on the back of the cards. Invent some fun new clothes for these people to wear. Make templates to see how the pieces go together. Glue and fasten as before. Add some glitter. Enjoy the party!

Pop-up Greetings

This pop-up card can be changed for many occasions. We made a frog, but you can easily make a Thanksgiving turkey or an octopus – they both have a beak!

You will need:

- *Thick drawing paper*
- *Colored markers*
- *Scissors, pencil, ruler*
- *Envelope*

25 MINUTES

What to do...

Fold a piece of thick paper, 16 x 19 inches (41 x 23 cm) in half, then in half again.

2 MINUTES

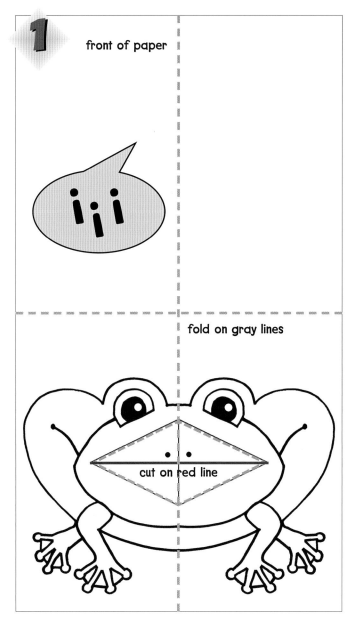

1 front of paper

fold on gray lines

cut on red line

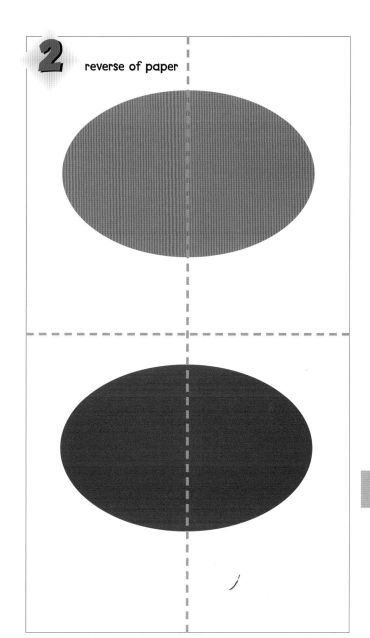

2 reverse of paper

21

3

Write your message in a speech bubble on the front.

Draw and color the frog. The mouth should be 5 inches (125 mm) long and go across the middle of the card. Draw the diamond-shaped fold lines. Open the page up and fold along these lines. Fold back along the long fold and cut the mouth line with scissors. Fold along the dotted lines for the upper and lower part of the frog's mouth. Open it up again, turn it over and paint the colors inside the mouth and allow it to dry. Fold the card again, this time making sure the mouth parts stick out so that the card closes with the mouth wide open.

Paper Weaving

Happy Birthday

Best Wishes

Can you find a picture in a magazine that you'd really like for a greeting card?
Here is a great way to give it the wow factor!

You will need:

- Thin card stock, white or colored
- Markers, pencil, ruler
- Colored magazine pictures
- Black and white photocopies
- Scissors, glue stick
- Envelopes

25 MINUTES

What to do...

Choose a color picture you like.
Find one with a clear image or pattern.

5 MINUTES

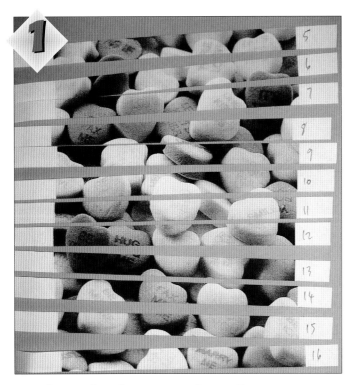

Cut the card to fit your envelope. Get a photocopy of your picture. Cut the copy side to side in .5-inch (12 mm) strips. Number the strips.

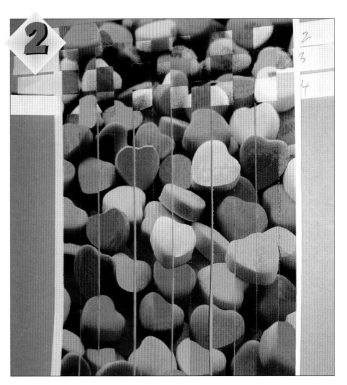

Make cuts .5 inch (12 mm) apart in the color picture but leave the top .5 inch (12 mm) connected. Glue the top edge down.

Start weaving the strips of the copy over and under the color picture, starting at the top.

Continue to weave the whole picture. Use the numbers to check that the strips are in the right order. Now just add your greeting.

Opposites

15
MINUTES

2
MINUTES

24

Using opposites is a really quick and effective way to make cards!
Stick with simple shapes and have fun.

You will need:

- *Colored paper*
- *Thin white card stock, pencil*
- *Scissors, glue stick*
- *Envelopes*

What to do...

Think of a simple design for your card, or copy ours. Notice that you only need to draw half of the shape. First, fold your white card stock and cut it to fit your envelope. We found a square envelope for our card, but you can change your design to fit the shape of your envelope.

1 Cut a shape in colored paper, half the width of your card. Draw half the shape in pencil.

2 Cut out the shape with scissors. Keep all the bits of paper together.

3

Glue a different-colored paper on your folded card as a background, leaving a narrow white edge. Glue down the right-hand side of your tree first, keeping it straight. Turn the cut-out shapes over and fit them together. Glue them in place. Put your personal message on the inside!

Try other designs using four sides.

Glitter and Glue

Exchanging cards is common at certain times of the year, especially at Christmas. By making drawings in glue and adding glitter, you can make your designs sparkle!

You will need:

- Colored paper or card stock
- Markers, scissors
- White glue
- Colored glitter
- Envelopes

35 MINUTES

What to do...

Fold and cut your cards to fit your envelopes. For Christmas you could find a real holly leaf to copy. For Halloween we have drawn a pumpkin with a face.

10 MINUTES

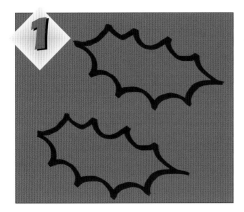

Draw two holly leaf shapes on some green paper.

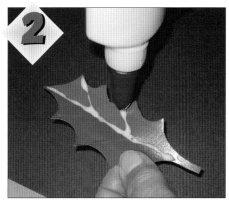

Cut the leaves out and use glue to draw in the veins.

Sprinkle glitter onto the wet glue and shake off the extra.

Glue the leaves on the card. Now put some glue and red glitter for berries!

Always allow the glue to dry completely before putting your card in the envelope!

More ideas for cards

- Snowman
- Snowflakes
- Christmas tree
- Presents in a stocking
- Santa Claus
- Easter bunny
- Halloween ghost
- Valentine hearts

Draw a pencil guideline or use glue directly on your card to make an outline of a pumpkin. Add the glitter and shake off the extra. Put in glue triangles for eyes and nose. Draw the teeth.

Shake on some more glitter. Let the glue dry. It's finished!

Write a greeting inside for your friends. They'll love the cards.

Hints and Tips: Work on a big sheet of paper so that you can collect all the dropped glitter for next time!

Pirates Ahoy!

Make this unusual card with a pirate theme. It's a complete adventure story in a card!

You will need:

- Colored papers, thin card stock
- Colored markers
- Fine black marker
- Scissors, paper, glue stick
- Large envelope

35 MINUTES

What to do...

A piece of A4 card stock is ideal for this project. Fold it in half, short side to short side, then fold again and again, making a zigzag, so you have eight sides.

5 MINUTES

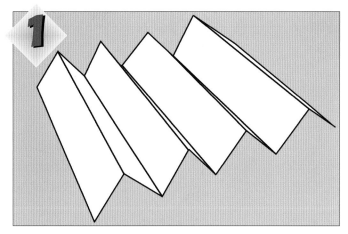

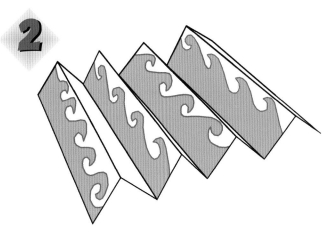

Look at the templates on page 30. Start with the sea at the bottom of the page. Trace or copy the shape onto blue paper. Cut along the wavy line to make two sets of waves.

Repeat this for four sets. Cut the sides to fit the card stock. The tops of the waves should be just below the folds. Stick them on the first, third, fifth and seventh faces of your zigzag card.

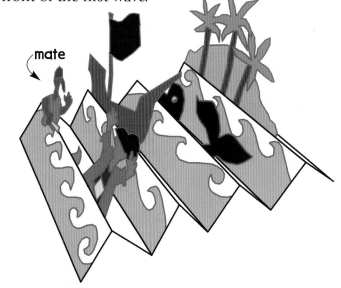

Choose the pirate captain from the templates. Cut him out in card stock and add colored paper for his clothes, or color him in with markers. Draw the details with a fine black marker. Glue the tab shown in yellow on the template.

Fix the tab to the back of the first zigzag. Glue the captain on the back of the first wave (see above). Glue the other cut-outs in place. The mate doesn't have a tab. Stick him on the front of the first wave.

Fix your card, so that the zigzag stands up. Fold it up to go in the envelope!

island

mate

whale tail

palm trees

pirate ship

whale

waves   shark fin   captain

Glossary

background   (BAK-grownd) The part of a picture that is behind the other part.

burnish   (BUR-nish) To smooth down a fold in paper with a tool, you can use a spoon or a ruler.

card stock   (KAHRD STOK) Like paper but thicker. It must be stiff enough for the card to stand up.

corrugated paper   (KOR-uh-gayt-ed PAY-per) A special kind of paper made from two pieces of paper with a wavy piece of paper glued between them. It can be bought in arts and crafts shops.

designs   (dih-ZYNZ) Plans for the form of something.

felt   (FELT) A thick soft cloth you can cut into shapes. It doesn't fray.

materials   (muh-TEER-ee-ulz) What something is made of.

paper fastener   (PAY-per FAS-ner) A small, two-pronged, metal piece used for fixing papers together.

pop-up card   (POP-up KAHRD) A style of card where a part of the card stands out from the fold.

rectangular   (rek-TAN-gyoo-lur) Like a square but longer one way than the other.

safety pin   (SAYF-tee PIN) A pin bent so that the point is guarded when closed.

Paper fastener

spongy cloth   (SPUN-jee KLOTH) A soft cloth, available in small squares for kitchen dishcloths.

stamp   (STAMP) A way of pressing a design onto paper using a pattern covered with paint.

tab   (TAB) A small piece of material connected to something.

template   (TEM-plut) Sometimes called a pattern, a template is a guide for making lots of things the same shape. There are some on the opposite page!

three-dimensional   (three-deh-MENCH-nul) Having height, width, and depth.

Index

Web Sites

Due to the changing nature of Internet links, PowerKids Press has developed an online list of Web sites related to the subject of this book. This site is updated regularly. Please use this link to access the list:

www.powerkidslinks.com/myoa/card/